IMAGES
of America

WASHINGTON
TOWNSHIP

Juanda

Thank you ♡

10/20/2019

Linda Osborne Gnowe

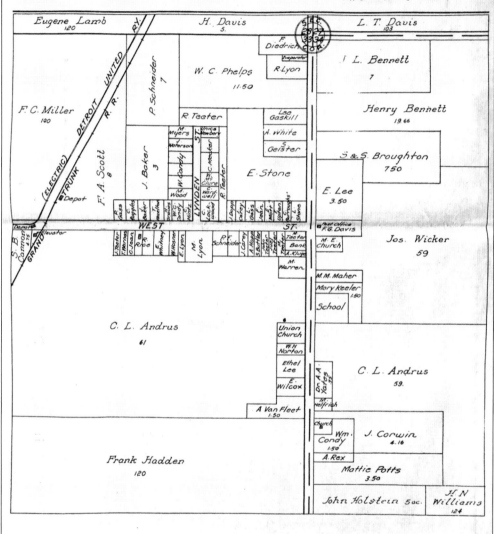

WASHINGTON

WASHINGTON TWP.

Copyright 1916 by Geo. A. Ogle & Co.

Pictured is a c. 1916 Washington Survey Map for Washington Village. (Courtesy of Greater Washington Area Historical Society.)

ON THE COVER: The Old Brick Schoolhouse was the first brick schoolhouse built in Washington, in 1839. Students are lining up for the picture taking event, where the photographer would capture a moment in time. The teacher standing with a book in her hand is Hettie M. Taylor. Principal Joseph Schnitzler is pictured at right in a suit and hat. (Courtesy of Greater Washington Area Historical Society and the John Gaskill Collection.)

IMAGES
of America

WASHINGTON TOWNSHIP

Linda Osborne Cynowa

ARCADIA
PUBLISHING

Published by Arcadia Publishing
Charleston, South Carolina

Printed in the United States of America

Library of Congress Control Number: 2019938111

For all general information, please contact Arcadia Publishing:
Telephone 843-853-2070
Fax 843-853-0044
E-mail sales@arcadiapublishing.com
For customer service and orders:
Toll-Free 1-888-313-2665

Visit us on the Internet at www.arcadiapublishing.com

*This book is dedicated to all the historians and archivists who work
so hard to keep the pieces of our past safe for future generations.*

*Learning is not attained by chance;
it must be sought for with ardor and diligence.*

—Abigail Adams

CONTENTS

ACKNOWLEDGMENTS

It is with the greatest appreciation that I thank Stacie Guzzo, branch manager and archivist, and Julie Oparka, branch specialist and archivist, of the Romeo District Library and Community Archives for their continued support, encouragement in the project, and unending help throughout this process. To Cherie Allen, historian at the Greater Washington Area Historical Society, for every one of my inquiries, an answer would always follow. Without their help, I doubt this book could have been written. I want to give with the greatest appreciation my thanks to the great people of the Greater Washington Area Historical Society (GWAHS), for all their help, including Pat Hallman and her historical expertise and Jim and Jean Holcomb. Many others were of help, including Jody Weymouth, Richard Daugherty, David McLaughlin, Betty Bucsek, Elizabeth Kane Buzzelli, Judy Gass Lopus, William Verellen of the Verellen Orchards, and Tim Smith, retired chief Gerald Alward and fire chief Brian Tyrell of the Washington Township Fire Department, pastor Phil Fitzgerald of the First Baptist Church of Washington, Margaret Kirsh from Our Redeemer Lutheran Church, Paula Klozik from SS. John and Paul Parish Church, the Washington Elevator staff, Friends of the Octagon House, and Richard Beringer and the Romeo Historical Society. To my daughter Brittany Cynowa, I can't thank you enough for the continued support, suggestions, and unending help given throughout this process. I give a special thanks to my title manager, Angel Hisnanick, for always having a great way of solving each and every issue I put before her. The majority of the images used in the book are individually credited, and to all those I did not mention above, I give my heartfelt thanks for permission to use these images to help preserve the history of Washington Township.

INTRODUCTION

Michi-Gan, as the early Indians called it, meaning the "Great Lake," was a land of blue waters, deep snow, and forests stretching to the horizon. In the beginning, it was a vast wilderness. The Chippewa, the Ottawa, the Huron, and the Potawatomi would become the first Michiganders and call this area home. In July 1805, land that was gained from the Indians in a treaty became the separate Territory of Michigan. On January 15, 1818, Macomb would be the third county to be organized by proclamation by Gov. Lewis Cass.

Sixteen miles northeast of Mount Clemens and 30 miles north of Detroit, it would soon bring many New Yorkers and New Englanders to the area called the village of Washington, so named when the organization of the new township was being discussed in the home of Alvin Nye on April 12, 1827. Daniel Thurston, one of a group of men at this meeting, said, "I move we name the town in honor of the father of our country." The name was accepted enthusiastically and would be confirmed by the act of organization. County organizers also created a township board, with Otis Lamb chosen as clerk. In one of their firsts acts as a board, members decided to raise $25 for support for the poor. During this time, the community had but 40 families. With that, the area became Washington Township.

Richard Jersey, the Brabb brothers (Isaac, George, and John), Elijah Thorington and son James, James Starkweather, and Elon Andrus were some, but not all, of the many settlers to put down roots in the area. Asahel Bailey would make the first entry of land in the township on July 3, 1821. By 1837, in less than 17 years, all the government-owned land in the township of Washington would pass into the hands of private citizens. There were 186 purchasers of land and, of those, seven were women: Ann Powell, Hannah Brabb, Dorcas Scott, Polly Graves, Mariah Millard, Joanna McDonald, and Lydia Inman.

William Austin Burt, one of the first settlers, was one of many who became a member of the territorial council, serving from 1826 to 1827, Burt moved to the legislature in 1853–1854. He was known as a mechanical genius and would rank high as an inventor. His principal inventions were a typewriting machine, the solar compass, and an equatorial sextant. Dr. Dennis Cooley, also an early settler, became a renowned botanist of record when he published his "List of plants common within ten miles of Cooley's Corners," which gave him much publicity as well as his classification of plants collected under the US Geological Survey in the Upper Peninsula in 1848. Dr. Cooley became one of the most noted botanists of his day.

Washington grew in the early years and became a thriving community with two churches, a well-organized school and hotel, and stores and businesses, including a general store run by Fred G. Davis. Before long, with Macomb County being situated on both the Grand Trunk Western Railroad and the Detroit United Railway (interurban line), doing business in the area was made all the more important to the farmers and orchard growers cultivating the rich soil so perfect for their crops. Historically, Washington Township has been a productive farming community, with a strong emphasis on its orchards. A significant part of the area is related to the beautiful orchards, still in business today.

In the northeast part of the town, where part of the village of Romeo is located, there was already a settlement forming. Several families of Indians lived there along with only a couple of white families. The location was then known as Indian Village or Hoxey's Settlement, where it is believed that Job Hoxey, soon after the surveys were made, moved with his family in 1820.

The village of Romeo is situated at the southeast corner of Bruce Township, a neighboring community to the north and extends into part of Washington Township to the south. Romeo was first plated in 1830, and would receive its name at that time, by the wife of one of the village proprietors, who thought it "classic, musical, short and uncommon." By 1836, log cabins were still predominant, with only about 30 frame buildings in town. The prosperous farming region that surrounded Romeo brought wealth into the settlement and soon permitted the villagers to indulge in the tasteful and unpretentious architecture for which the community is known.

Clifton, which was a platted village located near the intersection of 31 Mile Road and Mount Vernon Road, threatened to prove a dangerous rival to Romeo and may have eclipsed it had the railroad not decided to bypass Clifton and establish a route through Romeo. Clifton was the site of Grey's mills, which eventually became known as Clifton mills, did much business until about 1880 and help in the creation of a little settlement, with a church, a school, and a graveyard. The Grey family remained owners for some years, but in the 1890s the property passed to new proprietors. New processes have been put into the mill and the valuable waterpower is still used for the operation of a successful country mill.

Mount Vernon became a thriving village located in the southwest portion of Washington Township at Mount Vernon and 28 Mile Roads. It held a number of businesses, such as a general store, a cooper shop, a gas station, a rag-rug weaving shop, buggy shop, several sawmills, a greenhouse, two churches, a blacksmith shop, and a post office, which is considered one of the oldest post offices in the county. This community was almost instantly associated with William Austin Burt, who made his home in this area. On January 14, 1833, he received an appointment to be the first postmaster of Mount Vernon, which had then just been established, and in April of the same year, he was appointed associate judge of this judicial area. William also became one of the founding members of the Mount Vernon Baptist Church.

The Crissman, Clifton, Sikes, Thorington, and Hall Schools were all wood-frame, one-room schools houses, with Washington School being the first brick school in the village of Washington its self. These schools were built on land that was usually donated by the owners of the property or parents of the students.

There were eventually seven cemeteries in the community of Washington Township: Mount Vernon, Powell, Brabb, Washington South, Cannon, Clifton, and Washington Center, where most of the founding pioneering men and women of this community were laid to rest.

Beginning in the 1950s, much of the farmland was sold and converted to new home subdivisions, the one-room schoolhouses made room for brick and mortar buildings, and keeping the early history of the pioneering families alive fell to the wonderful and knowledgeable historians of the historical and archival societies that now work to protect this area's legacy.

One

VINTAGE WASHINGTON

Main Street is pictured at a busy time of the day in Washington, with the Washington Hotel that contains the E.A. Hinz Central Meat Market at the far left. This hotel was later replaced by the present-day Weir Block, the Davis Building and residence, and the Methodist church. (Courtesy of GWAHS and the John Gaskill Collection.)

Seen on the left in this view looking south on Main Street, the brick building is known as the Davis Building. Over the years, this structure would see many different establishments doing business there. This is at the crossroads of Main Street (now known as Van Dyke) and West Road. (Courtesy of GWAHS and the John Gaskill Collection.)

A short distance from the Davis Building is the First Methodist Church of Washington. The structure, with its foundation made of hand-hewn timbers with square nails and round wooden pegs, was built two years after the Methodist Episcopal Society of Washington was organized on November 25, 1842. (Courtesy of GWAHS and the John Gaskill Collection.)

The Washington Savings Bank, pictured around 1909, sat next to Dr. Dennis Cooley's house, south of West Road on the west side of Main Street. On January 7, 1929, two bandits robbed the savings bank of currency and $225.50 in gold, taking a total of $5,341.78. The case remained unsolved until January 28, 1929, when, according to the *Romeo Observer*, Thomas Sissions, 29, of Flint, better known as "Dapper Dan," was arrested in a Flint restaurant and positively identified, while the second robber continued to enjoy his liberty. In later years, the building was the home of Church & Church Lumber and later the Bank of Antiques, still operating today. (Both, courtesy of GWAHS and the John Gaskill Collection.)

Dr. Dennis Cooley was born February 18, 1790, in Deerfield, Massachusetts. He graduated from the medical college in Berkshire, Massachusetts, in August 1822. Dr. Cooley came to Michigan in 1827 and was described as being "of fine form, with a good mind and a little eccentric with his habits." (Courtesy of GWAHS.)

Dr. Cooley was among the few early physicians in the area, and his patients would come to the crossroads of West and Van Dyke Roads, which became known as Cooley's Corners. He developed a special interest in botany and went on to publish a "List of Plants Common Within Ten Miles of Cooley Corners." (Courtesy of GWAHS and the John Gaskill Collection.)

Dr. Cooley married Elizabeth Anderson in 1830, and they had two children who would not survive childhood. Elizabeth passed away in 1834, and the doctor remarried in 1836, to Clara Andrus, daughter of Elon Andrus. Dr. Cooley was also appointed postmaster for the village of Washington in 1836. After his appointment, the mail was carried by stagecoach from Royal Oak. For the next 23 years, Dr. Cooley attended to the mail, as well as to the sick from around the area, at his home. He continued to practice medicine until 1856, when he ceased due to his own illness. Dr. Cooley passed away on September 8, 1860. (Both, courtesy of GWAHS and the John Gaskill Collection.)

Dr. Albert Yates was born September 13, 1842, in Lincolnshire, England, and emigrated to Canada, where he obtained his early education. He then entered the Medical College of Detroit, graduating in 1872. After a short time in Canada, once again he came to Macomb County, in November 1872, and established a practice in the village of Washington. (Courtesy of GWAHS and the R.J. Brainard Collection.)

Dr. Yates married and was the father of five children. He became the secretary and treasurer of the Northeastern District Medical and Scientific Association in February 1876 and superintendent of schools for Washington Township. Dr. Yates continued to practice medicine until his death in 1929. This home was located just south of the present-day Washington Elementary. The house was torn down in 1971 because of its age. (Courtesy of GWAHS.)

The Washington Hotel is depicted as it appeared near the turn of the 20th century. The store at the left is the Washington Central Meat Market operated by E.A. Hintz. A sign advertises "Harness Repairing by Guss Kluge," who also used the hotel for his business. The town water pump is located to the left of the front porch. In 1868, J.M. Vaughan was known to be the proprietor of the Washington Hotel, but by January 1870 the hotel was advertised for sale or rent by owner S.A. Fenten. (Both, courtesy of GWAHS and the John Gaskill Collection.)

Through land grant transaction records, it is known that Elon Andrus (1786–1865) purchased this parcel of land in 1826 from John Bennett. It is believed the house was built between 1826 and 1839, as records for a frame schoolhouse built in 1839 refer to the location as opposite the Andrus house. (Courtesy of GWAHS and the John Gaskill Collection.)

This 1900 view of the east side of Van Dyke Road at the end of West Road shows the Central Meat Market owned by Frank Upton (standing in the front of the store) and the Davis store owned by Fred G. Davis. (Courtesy of GWAHS and the Virginia Bond Collection.)

F. G. DAVIS STORE and RESIDENCE WASHINGTON Mich. 1907

Fred Davis opened a store in the 1880s, soon after his marriage in 1883. By 1886–1887, he built the business block and an adjoining home in Washington. In 1916, the post office was located in Davis's store. He retired around 1922 and moved to Romeo, where he passed away in 1939. This store was later used as a restaurant and real estate office. The photograph was made around 1907. (Both, courtesy of GWAHS and the R.J Brainard Collection.)

In 1901, Lee Gaskill opened a barbershop in the Washington Hotel. Later, he moved into the building that formerly housed the Washington Central Meat Market, next to the Davis store. At the aptly named Lee Gaskill's Barber Shop, patrons could have a haircut and play a friendly game of pool. Later, this location became Duncomb's Drugstore. (Courtesy of GWAHS and the John Gaskill Collection.)

In this view looking west on West Road, toward the Washington Elevator and Interurban DUR Station and Durenberger's Store, an unidentified gentleman sits in the shade on a hot day. Many houses as well as a few businesses later lined this road, which became a major travel route for the people of Washington Township. (Courtesy of GWAHS and the Marlene Marsh Collection.)

Dated April 18, 1912, this postcard view of West Road just west of Van Dyke Road, on the south side of the street, shows the market built in 1910, where a little young lady waits patiently on a pony for someone to take her photograph while visiting the store. For a time, while C.J. Teeters owned it, the telephone exchange was located on the second floor. Later, the building housed Ernie's Tavern and Barber Shop, owned by Ernie Haase. Over the years, the location became a restaurant and a bar, with numerous owners. (Courtesy of GWAHS and the John Gaskill Collection.)

The view above faces east on West Road toward Van Dyke Road in 1908 and includes the post office and the back side of the Choppy Stone house. The Davis building as well as Davis's home are visible. The Washington Hotel is still standing in this view, but the Gaskill Barber Shop has been torn down and an empty lot left behind. The two-story building in the 1910 view below of the same street is now the Garland Agency. With the growth of the trees in the area, now long gone, West Street is not as noticeable as before. (Courtesy of GWAHS and the John Gaskill Collection.)

In this view looking down West Road toward the Davis Building on Van Dyke Road, the Powell House is shown at left. Many of these houses still stand on West Road today. (Courtesy of GWAHS and Marlene Marsh Collection.)

Main Street, also known as Van Dyke Road, is pictured in a view looking north. Many of these houses no longer exist, as their removal made way for business opportunities and progress along this still two-lane paved road. (Courtesy of GWAHS and the John Gaskill Collection.)

This view looking up West Street toward Mound Road shows what appears to be a quiet day when the Washington Elevator was accepting crops from the many farmers who would line up to bring them to and from the elevator. It is remembered as a time when long lines of teams, carts, and loaded wagons would line up as far back as the school on Main Street. The elevator had buildings where the crops, mostly potatoes and apples, were stored. (Both, courtesy of GWAHS and the Marlene Marsh Collection.)

This is the original Washington Elevator, pictured from West Road at the railroad tracks in Washington. Today, the elevator stands at the same site. The Washington depot can be seen at the left. Later, it was replaced by a larger station across the street. This view looks southwest and depicts the opposite side to the building below. This barn like structure was destroyed by fire and would be replaced. (Both, courtesy of GWAHS and the R.J. Brainard Collection.)

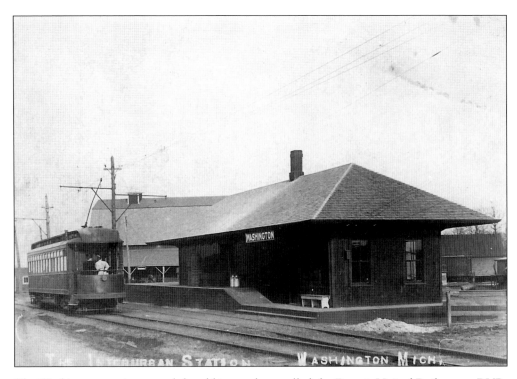

The Washington station served the old interurban, called the Detroit United Railway, or DUR, and often confused with the Grand Trunk Railway, whose tracks were located very close to those of the DUR. The Detroit United Railway was an electric train. After coming from Romeo into Washington, the line turned west to head toward the city of Rochester. It continued from Romeo into Almont and Imlay City. By 1934, all DUR lines were discontinued. Three workers pose for the camera, or they may be just waiting for the next train to arrive. (Both, courtesy of GWAHS and the John Burt Collection.)

The Washington Grand Trunk Depot was located on the north side of West Road and on the east side of the railroad tracks. Two young lads stand near the tracks, one posing for the photographer and the other in movement—and maybe in the process of throwing something at the direction of the photographer? (Courtesy of Romeo Community Archives, Romeo District Library.)

The Dernberger Store was located on West Road, east of the railroad tracks on the north side. The telephone exchange was located in the store at the time of this c. 1909 photograph. (Courtesy of GWAHS and the John Gaskill Collection.)

Florian Clark Miller became owner of the Miller farm after the death of his father, Hiram, in 1887. The younger Miller married Flora Lockwood, daughter of Timothy Lockwood of the same town, and together they had three children. The Millers were honored and highly respected. The Miller farm was located on West and Mound Roads. The home no longer stands. (Courtesy of GWAHS and the John Gaskill Collection.)

The building at 7687 West Street was home to the Washington Post Office for 35 years. The post office opened here around 1921, and in 1956 the services moved to the Weir Block, just around the corner on Main Street. Pictured from left to right are Herbert Singleton, Roy Lyons, Grover Powell, Nellie Powell, and unidentified. The date of this image is unknown. (Courtesy of GWAHS and the Marlene Marsh Collection.)

This view looks up 29 Mile Road west of Van Dyke Road, with the Haines farm on the north side of the street. The house stands today a part of the proud past of Washington, surrounded by today's progress of new construction. (Courtesy of GWAHS and the R.J. Brainard Collection.)

Nathan Keeler was born October 13, 1808, in New York. He came to Macomb County, Michigan, in 1833 and bought 120 acres of government-owned land in the Washington area. He lived there until 1850 and then purchased 160 acres of property off 28 Mile Road between Mound and Campground Roads on the north side of the street, where he built this home, where he lived—other than for two years when he resided in Romeo—until his death in 1869. (Courtesy of GWAHS and the Pat Hallman Collection.)

This south Main Street Victorian Gothic–style home was located between 26 Mile Road and the Octagon House. On the west side of Van Dyke, just north of the National City Bank, is the Lee Gaskill residence. Lee and Allie Gaskill are standing on the porch. Mr. Gaskill was known as the barber for Washington Township and had a shop on Van Dyke Road. (Both, courtesy of GWAHS and the John Gaskill Collection.)

Elisha Smith was born on May 13, 1807, in Warren County, New Jersey. He married Mary Tinsman on December 4, 1828, in Warren County, and they would have nine children in all. The Smiths came to Michigan in 1839 and settled in Washington on 160 acres on the west side of Mound Road between Inwood and 30 Mile Roads. After his death on March 14, 1875, Mary continued to live in the home with one of her daughters, Emma (Mrs. F.J. Crissman) and her family. The Smiths' double-wing Greek Revival home still sits on Mound Road today. (Both, courtesy of GWAHS.)

Elisha Smith
(DECEASED)

A 1917 view of the Bliss house shows Mrs. Bliss sitting on the steps and her sister standing on the porch. This postcard is dated June 19, 1917. (Courtesy of GWAHS and the John Gaskill Collection.)

South Main Street in Washington is pictured in this view looking north, with the house on the left at two blocks south of the light. (Courtesy of GWAHS and the John Gaskill Collection.)

Grover Powell's home was located at 1176 West Road, or Main Street (as it is often called). Powell was born in 1889, and Nellie Gass was born in 1892; they married in 1912 while living in Davis and moved to Washington in 1922. Mr. Powell was the township supervisor from 1932 until his retirement in 1955. He was also the owner of an insurance agency for over 27 years. Grover was 70 years old at his death in 1959. (Courtesy of GWAHS and the John Gaskill Collection.)

Joseph Sikes came to Michigan in 1831 from New York and purchased a farm in Washington in 1841. Known as a successful farmer with an unblemished character, Sikes passed away in 1878. His home was built on the southwest corner of Van Dyke and 30 Mile Roads, and the property was later known both as the Strong farm and East View Orchards. This site is now the home of the Huntington Bank. (Courtesy of GWAHS.)

Edwin Lamb built his house in 1860, on the farm just north of the fork made by Campground and Van Dyke Roads. Lamb was one of the famous quartet of homeowners that created a contest among themselves as to who could build the most impressive house in the township. This quartet included Lamb, Loren Andrus, Stephen Cannon, and Fred Miller. Two of the homes still stand: as the clubhouse of the Glacier Golf Club and the Loren Andrus Octagon House. The Miller and Cannon homes no longer exist. (Courtesy of GWAHS.)

Two

FARMING AND ORCHARDS

This aerial view looking north at the corner of Van Dyke and 29 Mile Roads during the 1970s shows the Verellen, Rapp, and Knittle Orchards. The Grand Trunk Railroad station has a then new home, now called the Whistle Stop and still within sight of the tracks that run through the area. (Both, courtesy of Romeo Community Archives, Romeo District Library.)

Roland W. Graubner was born in Fremont, Michigan, in 1904. Roland and Kathleen Eyer Rettenmier met when both worked on a bank merger, and on July 15, 1933, the couple married. Mr. and Mrs. Graubner had two children. In 1958, Roland and Kathleen moved from Detroit to Washington Township, where they spent their retirement years as fruit growers on their farm. (Courtesy of Melvin E. and Joan D. Bleich Collection, Romeo Community Archives, Romeo District Library.)

Roland Graubner's aunt Florence Brice owned the orchard along with her husband, Gideon. The orchard was located at 65885 Van Dyke Road. From 1933 till his retirement in 1969, he was employed by Detroit Bank and Trust, now known as Comerica Bank. Graubner rode daily into downtown Detroit to his job at the bank and home again each evening, when he would put on his overalls and work the orchard. (Courtesy of Melvin E. and Joan D. Bleich Collection, Romeo Community Archives, Romeo District Library.)

From 1969 till 1999, Roland Graubner served on the Romeo District Library Board. In 1970, he helped secure a federal grant for an addition to the Romeo Kezar Library by personally raising the money needed for the local share of the project. Graubner, along with his wife, Kathleen, would donate the 6.7 acres on Van Dyke Road between Romeo and Washington for construction of a new library building. In 1988, he was awarded the Michigan Library Association Citation of Merit Award, and 1991 would see him win the Macomb County Recognition Award. Graubner always felt everyone owed his or her community something. Roland Graubner passed away on July 21, 2000, at age 96. Kathleen Graubner passed away on September 18, 2000, at the age of 97. (Both, courtesy of Melvin E. and Joan D. Bleich Collection, Romeo Community Archives, Romeo District Library.)

In the early part of the 20th century, Frank Bowerman bought his apple and peach orchards on both the east and west sides of Van Dyke Road—between 30 Mile and 31 Mile Road. Bowerman, a baseball player for the New York Giants who played in the 1905 World Series, used his winnings to purchase the property. His wife, Pearl, and his son Thomas would continue farming the land. (Courtesy of Melvin E. and Joan D. Bleich Collection, Romeo Community Archives, Romeo District Library.)

Changes were later made to the property, and the peach trees on the east side of Van Dyke gave way to the Peachpit Lanes Bowling Alley. Additional land on the west side of Van Dyke Road was devoted to some peaches but mostly to apples. Here, Pearl Bowerman is working her stand on Van Dyke Road in 1987. She passed away at age 84 in 2003. (Courtesy of Melvin E. and Joan D. Bleich Collection, Romeo Community Archives, Romeo District Library.)

Henry and Lena Verellen and his brother and sister-in-law, Ed and Theresa Verellen, purchased 80 acres in 1920. There were 10 acres on Van Dyke Road and behind that, the other 70 acres on the east side of Van Dyke just east of the railway tracks along 29 Mile Road. Pictured are Henry Verellen and his son Robert. (Courtesy of Verellen Family Collection.)

An additional 20 acres were purchased during the 1940s. William and his wife, Ellen, took over from his father, Robert, and become third-generation fruit grows for Verellen Orchards in Washington Township, where they maintain a fruit and bakery shop year-round. (Courtesy of Verellen Family Collection.)

In 1931, East View Orchards was owned by Edward T. Strong, the president of General Motors' Buick Division. East View Orchards was one of the sponsors of the first festival. On Labor Day weekend, September 5–7, 1931, the first Michigan Peach Festival took place in Romeo. The peach queen and her court posed for photographs at Paton Hall at 124 West Gates Street. The court, from left to right, includes Ann Depuis, Margaret Mallory, Edith Levely, Helen Fortin, peach queen Virginia Allot, Traverse City cherry queen Maxine Weaver, Della Rickinger, Mary Fuller, Ilene Plassey, Alma Willard, and Helen Landon. The Peach Festival continues each year through the present day and is an important part of life for Washington-area orchards. (Both, courtesy of GWAHS.)

Edward and Grace Strong did not live at the farm, as their home was in Flint, Michigan. Fred and Josephine Scheuneman managed the farm for them from 1922 to about 1936. East View Farm was located on the southwest and southeast corners of Van Dyke and 30 Mile Roads, with the peach stand and farm buildings on the east side of Van Dyke, and the farm buildings located on the west side of Van Dyke. (Courtesy of GWATHS and the Dorothy Grace McClarty Collection.)

Southview Orchard owner Otto Knittle is preparing apples for sale on his farm. The Southview Orchard was located between 29 and 30 Mile Roads on Van Dyke Road. The Knittles purchased the property in 1933 and began cultivating the land for apple trees. Otto Knittle Jr. subsequently took over the property and cared for the fruit trees until the farm was sold in 1998. (Courtesy of Melvin E. and Joan D. Bleich Collection, Romeo Community Archives, Romeo District Library.)

Aaron Stone was born on June 30, 1790. He and his wife, Margaret Hayden Stone, came to Washington from Pittsford, New York, in 1822. They purchased 80 acres of government land at $1.25 an acre. That deed was dated July 10, 1823, and signed by Pres. James Monroe. The deed for an additional 80 acres purchased in 1826 was signed by Pres. John Quincy Adams. Their farmhouse began as a log cabin, and the Stones had a total of 10 children. In the early days, Indians would stop by for food and water. It is said in the family that Johnny Appleseed came through selling apple trees one year. Aaron Stone lived on and worked this land until his death in 1872. The farm then passed to his sons Arthur and Omar. (Courtesy of Melvin E. and Joan D. Bleich Collection, Romeo Community Archives, Romeo District Library.)

Sylvester Haines was born in 1847 in Shelby Township, Michigan. His grandfather Benjamin Haines purchased a farm on 29 Mile Road and cleared and improved the place, converting the wilderness into good cultivating land. After Sylvester reached his adulthood, he moved for a short time to Harvey County, Kansas. He later returned to Macomb County and in 1883 married Mary Haines of Monroe County, New York; they had one daughter. Sylvester purchased 80 acres near his grandfather's land and with his wife inheriting property, they owned a total of 182 acres that was placed under a high state of cultivation. He built a home and a substantial barn and with his general farming and stock raising, Sylvester became a success. The above photograph dates to around 1905, and the below image is from around 1967. (Both, courtesy of GWAHS and the R.J. Brainard Collection.)

James M. Thorington stands in front of the home of Roy Siglow, on Mound Road. He was born on January 26, 1837, in Washington, Macomb County, the son of James Thorington Jr. and Sally Brown. His father, James, would take up a farm, live there for about 30 years, becoming involved in agriculture and buying land. When he retired from active life, he owned 700 acres and was the first to import the Merino sheep from Vermont into Michigan. James M. Thorington would marry Mary Starkweather in 1857. They had five children together. James acquired an estate of 320 acres of first-class farming land on Mound Road between 30 and 31 Mile Road, with all modern equipment and conveniences, and would make a specialty of also raising pureblood Merino sheep, with a flock of over 100, and make sales to all parts of the country. He would cultivate a herd of Short-Horn Durham cattle and a brood of 11 Hambletonian horses. James passed away sometime in 1925. (Courtesy of GWAH.)

Built in the 1830s by the Lockwood family, the Lockwood house was located on the southwest corner of Mound and West Roads. In 1943, the home and farm were purchased by the Albert family, who sold the property in 1995, with the home demolished shortly afterwards. The 1916 photograph below, from an early 20th-century postcard, shows the Lockwood sheep farm, where the barns were located along the northwest corner of Mound and West Roads, section 32 of the Washington land grant map. (Both, courtesy of GWAHS and the Ronald Albert Collection.)

Samuel Barnes purchased two 40-acre parcels of government land on the north side of 27 Mile Road between Schoenherr and Hayes Roads on April 10, 1833. Horace A. Jenison bought the land from Barnes in March 1839, but Jenison only kept it until May 6, when Richard Carlton Jr. made a purchase of all 80 acres. Over the years, the farm was continued by Richard's son William, William's daughter Amelia (who married into the McClure family), and Amelia's daughter Ora (who married Benjamin Smith). The Smiths' son Leon would continue with the farm, and his son and daughter-in-law Tim and Karen Smith are still maintaining it as a working sesquicentennial farm today. Below, from left to right, are Benjamin Smith, Ora McClure Smith, Leon Smith (Tim's dad), Orie Smith, Orlo Smith, and Traveler. (Both, courtesy of Tim Smith Family Collection.)

James Thorington settled here in 1819 and built his home on Mound Road in Washington in 1830. It served as an inn for travelers who came to the area known then as the frontier. Referred to as the Thorington Inn, the building was located on a stagecoach route at the intersection of three roads and was often used by new settlers to the area. (Courtesy of GWAHS and the R.J. Brainard Collection.)

In 1890, George and Margaret Ticknell rented the farm once owned by the Thoringtons in Washington Township on Mound Road. After several years, they purchased the property and operated 200 acres of rich and workable land. The Ticknells also raised feed and sold stock. (Courtesy of GWAHS and the R.J. Brainard Collection.)

George and Margaret (Casey) Ticknell are pictured sitting in their carriage. George came to the Washington area in 1860 and married Maggie Casey of Romeo. They had four children over the years. During that time, they lived in Ray Township on rented land, which he farmed for three years; they then moved to Clinton Township, where George continued general farming for another three years. He soon found another tract of land, belonging the Elisha Smith, which in turn brought him to the land he called home. The residence would be torn down in 1991. (Courtesy of GWAHS and the R.J. Brainard Collection.)

Three

SCHOOLS AND CHURCHES

The Old Brick Schoolhouse, as it was known, was the first brick schoolhouse built in Washington, in 1839. There were two rooms in this brick building: one room to house the upper grades, with two wood-burning stoves, and the other room for the lower grades, where only one stove was used. In 1916, this building was demolished to make way for the new Washington High School. (Courtesy of GWAHS and the John Gaskill Collection.)

The students above were attending the Washington School in 1909. Many are lining up for the picture-taking event, and others are continuing their ball game, in spite of the photographer capturing a moment in time. The teacher standing with a book in hand is Hettie M. Taylor; the principal is Joseph Schnitzler. No date is given for this photograph. Below, a group of students has lined up for the class photograph in front of the soon-to-be-demolished Old Brick Schoolhouse. This is sometime before 1916 when the school was demolished. (Both, courtesy of GWAHS and the Margaret Ewalt Collection.)

The Washington School 10th-grade class picture in 1940 includes, from right to left, teacher Marsden Wilson, Donald Strose, Bill Alward, Roman Rogela, Mr. Joe (otherwise unidentified), Ora Weeks, Bud Danhouser, Ricky Woden, Delores Leonard, and Vivian Prey. Mr. Wilson was regarded as an exceptional teacher by many. (Courtesy of GWAHS and the John Gaskill Collection.)

The need was there, the citizens responded, and a school was built. The building was constructed to house three classrooms; two were 28 feet long and 23 feet wide; the other was 32 feet by 28 feet. All had 12-foot ceilings. These were all upper-level classrooms, with an auditorium in the downstairs. The school officially opened in January 1917. (Courtesy of GWAHS.)

The Washington High School baseball team photograph from 1912 includes, from left to right, (first row) Vern Dopp, George Thurston, and the team mascot; (middle row) Clare Thurston, Jay McMillian, Harley Dix, Lee Warren, Ralph Van Fleet, Burt Whitney, and Glen Holstein; (third row) Delia Alward, Helen Frost (Rath), Blanche Thurston, Marian Andrus, Joseph Schnitzler (principal, teacher, coach), Merle Glassford, Myrtle Hintz, and Hazel Teeters. (Courtesy of GWAHS.)

Pictured here at Washington High School in 1938 are, from left to right, (sitting) Marjorie Singleton, Mary Talaba, Marie Ramey, Laura Carleton, Betty Alward, and Marjorie Moore; (standing) teacher Mrs. Ratcliff, Robert Sword, Arthur Robertoy, Gordon Remple, Ivan Ware, and Marsden Wilson. (Courtesy of GWAHS.)

Washington School's seventh, eighth, ninth, and tenth grades are shown in this 1941 photograph. Identified from left to right are (first row) Betty Kage, Marjorie Sword, Rhea Prey, Eleanor Milhoff, Margaret Pierson, Shirley Alward, and Charlene Biddle; (second row) janitor Mr. Gooley, Janene Weeks, Ruth Steiner, Barbara Thurston, Pauline Leonard, Lila Langtry, Georgia Hughes, Vickie Meeker, Phyliss Moore, Kathleen Alward, Evelyn Weeks, and Dick Robb; (third row) Ray Weeks, Arnold Jamison, Walter "Dugan" Alward, Peter Hixon, Lester Green, Carl Durcha, Jack Robb, Ross Dawson, Tom Robb, Nelson Carleton, and teacher Marsden Wilson. (Courtesy of GWAHS.)

First-prize winners in the Washington School Hobby Show, held March 25, 1953, are shown here with their entries. From left to right are (first row) Ruth Ellen Walker, second grade; Kay Harris, first grade; and Patty McPeters, kindergarten; (center row) Linda Kleinow, sixth grade; Bill Nichols, third grade; and Sharon Hurdlow, fourth grade; (back row) Walter Koscierzynski, seventh grade; Hildegarde Gallert, fifth grade; and Dale Kiser, eighth grade. (Courtesy of Melvin E. and Joan D. Bleich Collection, Romeo Community Archives, Romeo District Library.)

The Sikes School is located on the northeast corner of Van Dyke and 30 Mile Roads. It is shown on a plate map from 1859, but no written records of the school exist prior to 1869. The white clapboard school was replaced in 1922 with a larger school, built on the same land, with the original building being moved across Van Dyke to the Bowerman property and restored. (Courtesy of GWAHS.)

In this c. 1917 image from the Sikes School are, from left to right, (first row) Charles Dodge, Armand Bowerman, Nellie Kuck, Mabel Johnson, Bernice Zielesch, Hazel Engel, Mary Dodge, Marguerite Schmidt, Ruthie Kuck, Stanley Sutton, and Elmer Lefever; (second row) Homer Lefever Lillian Squier, Evelyn Johnson, Lillian Zielesch, Hilda Schmidt, Helen Engel, Ethel Sutton, Walter Schmidt, and Daniel Frost; (third row) Ailene Ross, Ila Brandenburg, Eldon Sutton, Kenneth Inman, Byron Ross, Albert Kramer, and teacher Florence Brodie. (Courtesy of GWAHS.)

Louise Lock was the last teacher hired for the second Sikes School after consolidation in 1950. A vote to sell the schoolhouse was held in 1953. Only four votes were cast, all in favor of the sale. The building sold to Dr. David Roy of Romeo on June 6, 1953. It was converted into apartments and is still located on the original site. (Author's collection.)

The Thorington School is located on the west side of Mound Road just south of 31 Mile Road. The school has been in existence since the 1840s. James Thorington owned the 1/8-acre lot on which the school stands, with it being a part of his 158-acre farm. When the elder James Thorington died, his son James M. took over his farm and continued to lease the school property. On June 2, 1955, the school finally closed due to a need for consolidation. In the c. 1890 photograph above from the Thorington School, Mary Barnes is the teacher and the students, not listed in any order, are (girls) Mary Crissman, May Brabb, Eliza Crissman, Mina Crissman, Grace Thorington, Viola Lee, Lucy Lee, Mida Lamberston, Ann Lamberston, Carrie Cole, Clara Brabb, Julia Tincknell, and Josie Lamberston.; (boys) Walter Slating, Cassius Thorington, Walter Cole, and Vern Curtis. The neglected Thorington School is pictured below as it appears today. (Above, courtesy of GWAHS; below, author's collection.)

This 1925 Thorington School class photograph includes, from left to right, (first row) Kenneth Sutherland, unidentified, Gilbert Bossow, George Tincknell, Harry Tincknell, and unidentified; (second row) Stanley Falker, Gertrude Tincknell, Grace Lorraine Nunnely, Thelma Tincknell, Louis Falker, Ruth Tincknell, and Dorothy Siglow; (third row) Marion Tincknell, Arlene Siglow, Helen Siglow, Helen Sutherland, Jean Siglow, Lydia Falker, and Marion Nunnely; (fourth row) Roy Siglow, Don Tincknell, Floyd Siglow, and Daisy White. (Courtesy of GWAHS and the Clare Tincknell Collection.)

This 1931 Thorington School class photograph includes, from left to right, (first row) James Stuart, Edgar Stuart, Ford Stuart, Howard Falker, and two unidentified; (second row) Florence Siglow, unidentified, Leone Tincknell, three unidentified, Thelma Tincknell, and Nonda Tincknell; (third row) unidentified, Edward Sutherland, Gertrude Tincknell, Dorothy Stuart, unidentified, and Ruth Tincknell; (fourth row) Marty Falker, unidentified, Raymond Stanaback, Roswell Stuart, Mrs. Snyder (teacher), Ethylene Bossow, and Ruth Tincknell. (Courtesy of GWAHS and the Clare Tincknell Collection.)

The Crissman School was located on the west side of Mound Road just south of 29 Mile Road. The school opened in 1851, but it was replaced during the summer of 1869 by a new schoolhouse measuring 38 by 28 feet that sat on a rock foundation. The schoolroom had a very high ceiling, a single door for entry, and a furnace in the right corner. The former school now is part of a home on 28 Mile Road. (Courtesy of Elizabeth Kane Buzzelli.)

This photograph was taken at Crissman School in 1952, just before Christmas. Pictured from left to right are (first row) Kathleen Bliss, Roger Heitmeyer, Mary Ross, Linda Kuhn, and Noreen Wethy; (second row) James Anderson, John Vaginas, Carl Heitmeyer, Gretchen Kuhn, Billy Stefanski, and Harry McDonald; (third row) Welsey Kuhn, Herbert Bliss, Sandra Stefanski, Diane Kuhn, John Ross, and teacher Florence Werdman. (Courtesy of Elizabeth Kane Buzzelli.)

The Washington Union Church was originally built in 1879. It was used in the first half of 1916–1917, when classes were held in the church dining room for three months while the new high school was being built. It stopped serving as the Union Church in 1937. But the structure found itself home to services again for a number of community churches looking for their permanent homes. (Courtesy of Romeo Community Archives, Romeo District Library.)

The First Baptist Church conducted services here until 1943, and Redeemer Lutheran Church would hold services at this structure in 1947; by that time, the church building became a men's club. With some structural changes, the building became the home of many businesses over the years. It was located on Van Dyke Road between West and 26 Mile Roads. (Courtesy of GWAHS and the R.J. Brainard Collection.)

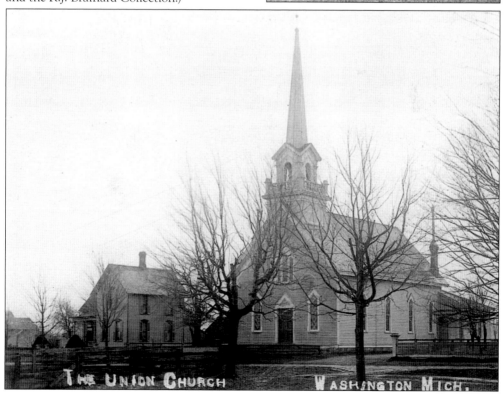

In the contract signed between the builder and church members paying for the building costs, under the date February 12, 1846, the following statement was recorded: "The trustees for the first Methodist Episcopal Church in Washington, was contracted to Chauncey Church to build a meeting house for the M.E. Church on the west side of Section 24, in Washington Township, with the said house to be 36 x 50 feet, without a belfry, to be finished by the first day of January 1847, for the sum of $1150.00." Elon Andrus, Abel David N Noyes and John Keeler signed this contract for the church members. The inside the Methodist church is pictured in 1908. (Above, courtesy of Romeo Community Archives, Romeo District Library; below, courtesy of Melvin E. and Joan D. Bleich Collection, Romeo Community Archives, Rome District Library.)

A belfry was added, and a bell was donated in 1854. After further renovation, the church was rededicated on January 30, 1878. By that point in the church's history, it had already been over 50 years since Elon and Nancy Andrus, Polly Greene, John Holland, and Aurilla and Laura Miller formed the first "class" of Methodists in Washington in 1823. (Courtesy of GWAHS.)

The four-alarm fire that leveled the 36-by-50-foot church on December 17, 1953, may have been caused by sparks from a chimney cleaning or a short circuit in the electrical box located in the rear of the building. A cornerstone-laying ceremony for a new church took place in November 1954. (Courtesy of GWAHS and the John Gaskill Collection.)

It was a very cold day in January 1956 when a dozen or more men worked on a three-acre parcel of land along Van Dyke Road in Washington to make a 13-year dream come true for the First Baptist Church. The long history began in 1940 in the home of Vaughn and Grace Greene. The church was able to use the Washington Union Church on Van Dyke Road until 1943. Members then purchased the Weir Block in 1944, and the building was remodeled to provide an auditorium on the main floor and living quarters upstairs. The church's present location was purchased in 1954, and a dedication was held on October 7, 1956. The First Baptist Church had a number of renovations over the next years, with work continuing as it supports 120 missionaries around the world. (Above, courtesy of Melvin E. and Joan D. Bleich Collection, Romeo Community Archives, Romeo District Library; below, author's collection.)

The name chosen was SS. John and Paul Parish. The territorial area extended from Romeo Plank Road to Dequindre Road, 26 Mile Road, and 30 Mile Road. Services were first held in the homes of parish members, but they were soon moved to Powell Junior High School. A desire grew for their own church building led parishioners to form a committee. The ground-breaking in October 1983 was on land that the Archdiocese of Detroit had owned for some years, on 28 Mile Road west of Campground Road. In 1984, bids were made for construction of the church, revisions were made, an architect was hired, and a site plan was completed. With the church building finished, the parish continued to grow and thrive in the community. (Both, courtesy of SS. John and Paul Parish Collection.)

The first worship services for Our Redeemer Lutheran Church were held on June 15, 1947, in the men's club building, formerly the Union Church of Washington on Van Dyke Road, which stopped its own services in 1937. Rev. Paul Heinecke conducted that first Lutheran service. By 1949, seven acres on 27 Mile Road was purchased for $2,400 for the new church site. The dedication of Our Redeemer Lutheran Church was held on July 22, 1951. In 1957, construction began on a new parsonage, with 1959 seeing a new educational wing built. By 1967, there was a need for a larger space for services, and plans were soon adopted. In 1983, the Little Lambs Preschool began; it continues to run through the present day. (Courtesy of Melvin E. and Joan D. Bleich Collection, Romeo Community Archives, Romeo District Library.)

Four

THE WASHINGTON OCTAGONS

A northern view shows the Loren Andrus Octagon House. Andrus, with the help of his brother-in-law David Stewart, started the building in 1858. It was completed in 1860. The house is located on the east side of Van Dyke Road just north of 26 Mile Road. (Courtesy of GWAHS.)

The Octagon House is a two-story, eight-sided brick structure. The roof has extravagant Italianate supporting brackets and an octagonal cupola with weatherboard sheathing on top. A large porch supported by wooden Neo-Corinthian columns wraps around seven sides of the house. The home has three-foot-thick walls in the basement and 15-inch-thick exterior walls. (Above courtesy of GWAHS; below, courtesy of the Friends of the Octagon House.)

In the interior, the house has four rooms on each level. In the center of the structure is a dramatic staircase that extends upward from the main floor all the way to the cupola. There are 12-foot ceilings and eight-foot windows throughout the first floor, and 11-foot ceilings with six-foot windows on the second floor. The rooms were equipped with iron stoves for heating. Next to each room is a triangular alcove, making hallways unnecessary. There were 16 rooms with a total living space of 3,200 square feet. (Both, courtesy of Friends of the Octagon House and author's collection.)

The idea for a farm college campus came from a Detroit businessman by the name of Albert H. Schmidt. Schmidt donated the money to purchase the Octagon House and surrounding farm property for what became known as the Albert H. Schmidt Experimental Farm of Wayne State University. (Courtesy of GWAHS and the John Gaskill Collection.)

The Albert H. Schmidt Foundation of Wayne State University's intent was to teach soldiers returning from war about the trade of farming—and later inner-city children about modern farming and becoming self-sustaining. After 19 years of ownership, the foundation sold the home and 323-acre farm site in the spring of 1964. (Courtesy of Friends of the Octagon House and author's collection.)

For some years after the sale, the property was rented or leased to a number of tenants who would farm the land. In 1971, the Octagon House was placed on the National Register of Historic Places, and in 1972 it was recognized as a State of Michigan Historical Site. By the late 1980s, the Save the Octagon House group was formed; in April 1989, the organization changed its mission statement and became Friends of the Octagon House, with the intention of restoring the Octagon House and opening it as a living museum. (Both, courtesy of Friends of the Octagon House and author's collection.)

Wells Burt (1820–1887), son of William Austin Burt, was born in Wales Center, Erie County, New York. His life's work was exploration and the promotion of iron and other industries. Wells's father instructed him in land surveying, and Wells was engaged by the State of Michigan to survey public lands in northern Michigan. He died in Detroit, Michigan, on November 29, 1887. (Courtesy of GWAHS and the John Burt Collection.)

The construction of this house was different than that of the Andrus Octagon House, as it was not necessary to make the walls the same thickness because of the structure being clapboard in style. The Wells Burt Octagon house originally sat on 75 acres. The farm was mainly home to dairy farming and the raising of sheep. (Courtesy of GWAHS.)

In 1843, William Austin Burt (1792–1858), a renowned inventor and farmer, built this house in an octagonal design for one of his sons, Wells Burt. The home was a standout, with a veranda on the second story that went around the entire house and included approximately 300 spindles. Its exterior was full clapboard. The Burt house would have a narrow straight stairway to the second floor. There were approximately 2,400 square feet with 11 rooms, 6 of them triangular. This house predates the Loren Andrus Octagon House by 17 years. (Both, courtesy of GWAHS and the Pat Hallman Collection.)

It was during the years of 1844 through 1846 that William Austin and three of his sons—Austin, Wells, and William—moved their families to new homes they built in Mount Vernon, While Wells Burt only lived in his home, located next door to his father's home, for just over a decade, it was during an important time in his life. (Courtesy of GWAHS.)

Five

VILLAGE OF ROMEO

The May 5, 1869, *Romeo Observer Press* reported, "The north half of the village of Romeo lies in the township of Bruce. In it there is not a hotel, saloon, groggery, and billiard table or ball alley. The south half of the village lies in the township of Washington. In it there are three hotels, three or more saloons, and six billiard tables, and three of those are newly fitted over Larzalier's Store." (Courtesy of Judy Lopus Collection.)

The Welcome to Romeo signs that greet visitors and residents alike at the four entrances to Romeo undergo extensive face-lifting every five years or so, always in time for the Peach Festival that takes place each Labor Day weekend. Bob Owen, a Romeo sign painter, does the renovating work sponsored by the Rotary and Lions Clubs. (Courtesy of Melvin E. and Joan D. Bleich Collection, Romeo Community Archives, Romeo District Library.)

Approximately 60 members of the Romeo High School Band made the trip up to Traverse City, Michigan, each year to march in the Traverse City Cherry Festival Parade. Each year, funds were raised by a combination of a bake sale and tag day that was sponsored by the bandmembers. The trip usually took three days, and often included a side trip to the National Music Camp at Interlochen. (Courtesy of Melvin E. and Joan D. Bleich Collection, Romeo Community Archives, Romeo District Library.)

In the early days of Romeo, the village was a far cry from the clean, orderly community known today. In 1836–1837, the streets were encumbered with stumps, and travelers were brought to a standstill—especially at night. Even though the roads were not always passable and cleared, a one-day mail service between Romeo and St. Clair was offered. The Detroit United Railway, or DUR, placed tracks down the middle of Main Street, with a turn west onto St. Clair Street, then on to Prospect and a run through to Imlay City. Years later, when the DUR stopped service in the mid-1930s, the tracks were removed and cars took the place of horses and buggies. (Both, courtesy of Judy Lopus Collection.)

J.D. Elliott was the proprietor of the American Hotel, built in the early 1860s, and he took possession of the property and commenced business by April 1870. Elliott's plans were to keep a first-class hotel, and he put $1,300 worth of repairs into the building. The structure was built of brick and had a wood front portion with a long front porch. It was located on the west side of South Main and West Lafayette Streets. By the early 1900s, the building was all brick and had a two-story porch as seen in these photographs. By this point in time, it was call the Romeo Hotel. The structure was be torn down in 1960. (Both, courtesy of Judy Lopus Collection.)

The First Baptist Church of Romeo was located on South Main Street in Romeo and was built in 1853 in the Greek Revival style at a cost of $2,228 for the church and $800 for the parsonage next door. The spire was blown off in a severe storm in 1934 and was not replaced. The building had other uses in later years. (Courtesy of Melvin E. and Joan D. Bleich Collection, Romeo Community Archives, Romeo District Library.)

The Little Red Mill is one of Romeo's oldest landmarks and was the first home of the *Romeo Observer*. The mill was built by Samuel Holdbrook Ewell and Irving Hanscomb and the Ewell family. S.H. Ewell bought the *Observer* in 1869 and sold it in 1874. The paper was printed here for only a short time. Samuel's son Leon sold the mill in 1944. In its last few years, the building served as a feed store before being razed in 1950. (Courtesy of Romeo Historical Society.)

Clyde Craig opened a blacksmith, farrier, fur-trading station, veterinarian's office, and wheelwright shop in 1920. The structure began as a carriage barn, became a tinsmith, an upholstery shop, and an auto repair shop before Clyde purchased it. In 1972, after Clyde Craig had passed away, the building was moved from its original spot on Bailey Street east of St. Clair Street to North Main Street to be renovated as a living historical site. The image below is from a postcard used to promote the museum. (Both, courtesy of Melvin E. and Joan D. Bleich Collection, Romeo Community Archives, Romeo District Library.)

The Romeo Electric Light Plant, also known as the Water Works Building, generated the electricity for the village. Located on East St. Clair and Railroad Streets, it was built in the early 1900s out of brick. As the years passed, changes to the roofline and the removal of the chimney changed its appearance somewhat. The structure still stands today. (Both, courtesy of Romeo Historical Society.)

May 30. 1907. just got home from down town Romeo is dead to what it use to be

Have you heard that Wm Hildenbrand is dead? she died last Friday, she had an operation last Wednesday, was to bad.

George Washington Brabb was a prominent farmer and businessman with investments in a hardware store and implement business. He fostered numerous local industries and contributed his means and influence to benefit the people of Romeo and Macomb County. In 1877, Brabb built his Italianate home, located on South Main Street. Many consider it to be one of the most sophisticated homes in Romeo. (Courtesy of Judy Lopus Collection.)

Isaac Crawford, a native of New Jersey, arrived in Romeo in 1850 and worked for the Snover and Bellows Blacksmith Shop for a few years before establishing a blacksmith shop of his own. He built his Victorian Gothic home in 1870 and added a Queen Anne porch in early 1900. This home today is located on Tillson Street. (Courtesy of Romeo Community Archives, Romeo District Library.)

Asahel Bailey arrived in Indian Village in January 1821. In July of that same year, he purchased 80 acres of government land on 26 Mile Road at Van Dyke. Bailey settled in Romeo early on. In 1858, he built his Greek Revival residence at 343 South Main Street (Van Dyke Road); this was his third home in the area. A writer for the *Romeo Observer* in 1871 commented, "Ashael Bailey was the pattern farmer of the settlement. His fields were always we cleaned and finely cultivated. His buildings were in good condition, his fences in good repair, his stock always in good order and his harvests bountiful." After use as the parsonage for St. Clement and a Pontiac Nursery office, Bailey's former house was moved and became a private home once again. (Courtesy the Romeo Community Archives, Romeo District Library.)

The village of Romeo was originally called Indian Village, as the Chippewa Indians first called this area home. The village sits right within the northern boundary of Washington Township at 32 Mile, or what the locals call St. Clair Street. Many of the farming property owners built their homes in the community (village). Romeo is well known for its Peach Festival, held every Labor Day weekend since 1931. (Courtesy of Romeo Community Archives, Romeo District Library.)

Six

THE VILLAGES OF CLIFTON AND MOUNT VERNON

Clifton is an unincorporated community near the intersection of 31 Mile Road and Mount Vernon Road. The Gray brothers of Romeo purchased two mills: The Clifton mill, lower downstream, and the mill at Lakeville farther upstream. Controlling the water between the two mills was important. The mill operated from the mid-1800s into the 1970s, and it is still privately owned. (Courtesy of Romeo Community Archives, Romeo District Library.)

Clifton Mill is pictured in the mid-1940s, around the time the Weymouth family purchased the mill and surrounding land. The old mill is also one of the remaining pieces of history related to Clifton Village. It was used as a general store and office back when the area was still a village. Clifton later became known as a lost village when the railroad was built east of Romeo. (Courtesy of Lawrence and Jody Weymouth Collection.)

James Keel was born in 1821 in Somersetshire, England. He emigrated to America with his family in 1830. In 1838, he came to Clifton and worked in the Clifton Mill until it was destroyed by fire in 1844. Romeo once again became his home in 1873; and he once again became employed at the Clifton Mill after Hugh and James Gray had it rebuilt. (Courtesy of Lawrence and Jody Weymouth Collection.)

Once upon a time, there was a proper mill wheel, whose turning produced the power that made possible the mill's product, a natural flour; but many years ago, the wheel was replaced with a turbine, now hidden from view. Lawrence B. Weymouth and Cletus Hunt are pictured fixing the buhrstone shipped from France that had served in the grinding process since the mill was founded. (Courtesy of Lawrence and Jody Weymouth Collection.)

Cletus Hunt, the slight, smiling miller, was the one who bought and received the grain from the farmers, put it through the cleaning and grinding process of the mill, did the packaging (about 600 small bags a week), and then delivered it to the stores. If nothing went wrong, he could mill about one and half tons a week. (Courtesy of Lawrence and Jody Weymouth Collection.)

Since the late 1970s, when normal production stopped, the mill has operated every three years in order to retain legal rights to the water from Stoney Creek. Three bags of corn are cracked by the milling equipment, and a notary public is on hand to witness the signing of the documentation. (Courtesy of Lawrence and Jody Weymouth Collection.)

Owner Lawrence Weymouth shows manager Cletus Hunt various packages of grist flour and the many different types of flour the mill could produce, as in graham flour, rye and buckwheat flours and even a pancake mix, among many other types. (Courtesy of Lawrence and Jody Weymouth Collection.)

A successful professional man, Lawrence Weymouth would drive around exploring with his wife and son. Several miles from Romeo, they would see the Clifton Mill, located along Stoney Creek, with a rushing stream of water flowing under it. The old building still stood proudly by the roadside. A few inquiries and some judicious bargaining would find Lawrence Weymouth the owner of a century-old mill, with its original buhrstone grinding wheels. Below is a mid-1940s view of Lawrence looking over the dam that fed the mill. (Both, courtesy of the Lawrence and Jody Weymouth Collection.)

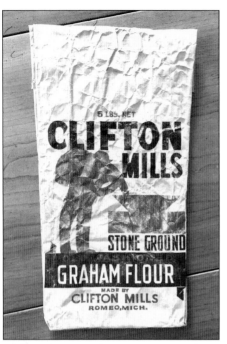

The flour was carried on the shelves of many stores in colorful grey, red, and blue Clifton Mills sacks, whose design did not change much within anyone's memory. The retail stores at times complained of the difficulty in getting enough of the flour as it went out the door so fast. (Courtesy of Lawrence and Jody Weymouth Collection.)

Lawrence and Marion Weymouth purchased the mill around 1945 and saw flour and cornmeal sold as a higher grade product throughout the region, at retailers such as A&P and Hudson's. The mill last operated commercially in 1977, but the entire building has been maintained and lovingly preserved by Lawrence and Marion's son and daughter-in-law Lawrence Jr. "Butch" and Mary Jo Weymouth and their family ever since. (Courtesy of Lawrence and Jody Weymouth Collection.)

Clifton School was located on Dequindre Road a quarter-mile north of 31 Mile Road. With the first school building most likely having been built in the 1830s when the village of Clifton was first settled, it was well established by 1859. During World War II, the government delivered food daily and the teacher prepared lunches for the students. The year 1949 would be the last the building was used as a school for students, and it was then offered for sale in 1953, with the bell going to the last teacher, Mrs. Parsons—purchased for her by a group of her former students. Here, in May 1948, Mrs. Walter Parsons greets Charlene Hobbs and Allene Bugenski, Romeo High School students returning to enjoy the picnic reunion. (Right, courtesy of the Melvin E. and Joan D. Bleich Collection, Romeo Community Archives, Romeo District Library; below, courtesy of GWAHS.)

The Clifton Cemetery is located on Dequindre Road between 31 and 32 Mile Roads in Washington Township. There might be as few as 27 people buried there, with the cemetery being part of what was known then as the village of Clifton. According to the grave markers, the first burials could have been as early as 1837 or 1838. After the railroad made its way into Romeo, the community no longer continued to thrive. The last known burial was in 1892. (Both, author's collection.)

One of the many early homes in the community is seen in Mount Vernon, which included the Mount Vernon School, Fangboner Buggy Shop, the General Store with a post office, and two churches. The times changed when Mount Vernon was bypassed by the railroad. The Methodist church and the cemetery are all that is left of the so-called four corners. This home on Mount Vernon Road is just south of 28 Mile Road and still stands today. (Courtesy of GWAHS and the Pat Hallman Collection.)

Mount Vernon Baptist Church was located on the west side of Mount Vernon Road and south of 28 Mile Road. William Austin Burt helped start this church and he and his family worshipped there. It was built in the late 1840s and was razed in the 1920s. (Courtesy of GWAHS and the John Burt Collection.)

In 1858, a pastor was sent to Mount Vernon as a missionary, as the remote areas of Mount Vernon, Rochester, and Stoney Creek were referred to as "waste places" by 19th century historians. In 1870, Rev. I. Johnson was appointed, and soon after church socials were organized to raise the $2,000 it would take to build the church at the corner of 28 Mile and Mount Vernon Roads. The acre of land the church sat on cost $200. The original name was Mount Vernon Methodist Episcopal Church, but by 1969 it was called Mount Vernon United Methodist Church. (Both, courtesy of GWAHS and the Pat Hallman Collection.)

This sketch depicts William Austin Burt, born in Petersham, Massachusetts, on June 13, 1792. Burt acquired much of his knowledge from borrowed books read by the light of a burning pine knot. He became a millwright, surveyor, and inventor to support his family. Burt passed away in 1858 in Mount Vernon, and he was interred in Detroit's Elmwood Cemetery. (Courtesy of GWAHS.)

HON. WM. A. BURT.

William Austin Burt's home, seen in this c. 1909 image, was built in 1840 on 28 Mile Road just east of Mount Vernon. This is one of four houses William Burt built in the Mount Vernon community, and this was the one he lived in during his time here. (Courtesy of GWAHS and the John Burt Collection.)

The William Burt home was located on Mount Vernon Road just south of Snell Road. The house was built in the 1840s by William's father, William Austin Burt. It was destroyed by fire after being struck by lightning in the 1960s. (Courtesy of GWAHS and the John Burt Collection.)

The Austin Burt house is located on the southwest corner of 28 Mile and Mount Vernon Roads. From a postcard taken around 1909, this image shows one of a number of clapboard homes that William Austin Burt built for his sons and their families. (Courtesy of GWAHS and the Pat Hallman Collection.)

In 1809, William Austin Burt devised a system of shorthand to aid in more rapid note-taking, but letter writing could never be simplified. Unlike many who invent for wealth, William invented the first typewriter out of a genuine need to resolve a problem. Many of the parts and tools were forged in his own workshop. But William would complete a crude and simple machine. The mechanism was housed in a small wooden box measuring 12 inches wide, 12 inches high, and 18 inches long. On July 23, 1829, Pres. Andrew Jackson signed the Letters Patent for William's Typographer. For the next 14 years, William Austin had "the full and exclusive right of making, constructing, using and vending to others" America's first writing machine. The Mount Vernon General Store was at first a two-story inn. In the early days, the post office was in the corner of the store, which had numerous owners over the years. It was located on the northeast corner of the main intersection. (Both, courtesy of GWAHS and the John Burt Collection.)

Austin Burt (1818–1894) became a surveyor like his father, and much of his work was in the Upper Peninsula of Michigan. The homes built by William Austin were known as the "Burts' chalets." Although the Burts only lived in the chalets for a decade, these were their homes during an important time in their lives. (Courtesy of GWAHS and the John Burt Collection.)

Austin Burt had a blacksmith shop and wagon shop located on the northwest corner of 28 Mile and Mount Vernon Roads in Mount Vernon. It is seen here around 1909. (Courtesy of GWAHS and the John Burt Collection.)

The Mount Vernon Cemetery is located at 28 Mile and Mt. Vernon Roads. It was part of what was then the village of Mount Vernon, an unincorporated township. The cemetery was organized in 1841, but it was known to have burials some years earlier. Many pioneering families, with names like Crissman, Flummerfelt, Fangboner, and Axford, were buried there. One of Washington's most famous pioneers and one of the prominent citizens of the Mount Vernon area, William Austin Burt, who died in 1858, was originally buried in Mount Vernon Cemetery, but in 1888 he was reinterred in Detroit's Elmwood Cemetery with other Burt family members. (Both, author's collection.)

Charles C. Crissman, born November 10, 1820, to parents Benjamin and Mary Crissman, went on to become one of the most prosperous agriculturists in Washington Township. Charles built his home on 160 acres on the south side of 28 Mile Road west of Mound Road. Charles married Laura Parrish in 1853, and they had six children. Laura Crissman was the first teacher in the Crissman School. There once were 32 Crissmans enrolled at the same time. Charles passed away on January 15, 1902, and was buried in the Mount Vernon Cemetery. (Author's collection.)

Seven

WASHINGTON'S CEMETERIES

The Cannon Cemetery occupies a strip of land 140 feet wide adjoining the Washington South Cemetery, along its north, south, and eastern boundaries. It was originally landscaped with one 80-foot-diameter mound to contain burials and grave markers, plus a central monument to display all the names and dates. The remaining vacant areas are reserved for future burials of those who can establish a Cannon blood relationship. (Author's collection.)

This column is made of granite and limestone, with a height of 12 feet, and cost $1,500. The layout of the cemetery is very similar to that of the National Cemetery at Gettysburg, Pennsylvania. Irving D. Cannon (1866–1953), pointing at the monument he was so proud of, passed away at nearly 87 years of age in Santa Rosa, Texas. Upon his death, his body was returned to Michigan and rests among his ancestors. (Courtesy of GWAHS.)

The Cannon Cemetery is located along 26 Mile Road, east of Mound Road. The Alexander Macomb Chapter of the Daughters of the American Revolution now owns the cemetery, together with its endowment, and is responsible for providing in perpetuity supervision, maintenance, and proper use and care. (Author's collection.)

Elon and Nancy Andrus are buried in Washington South, along with two of their sons: Loren, best known for having built the Octagon House, and Truman, who followed his father in the development and expansion of their farming operations. Both Loren and Truman were charter members of the Agricultural Society of Macomb County. (Author's Collection.)

The Washington South Cemetery is located on the northeast corner of 26 Mile and Mound Roads. Earlier on, it was called the Chapman Cemetery, after early pioneer John Chapman. Burials seem to have started as early as 1826 and would continue into the 1970s. Many pioneering names such as Andrus, Lockwood, Cooley, and Yates as well as many military men are buried in this small cemetery. (Author's collection.)

Many prominent individuals of Washington Township were buried here, with family names of Powell, Jersey, Nims, Rood, and Graubner among them. It is thought that Hiram Anderson was buried here in 1810, in what may very well be the oldest grave in Washington Township. (Author's collection.)

The Powell Cemetery is located on Powell Road between 30 and 31 Mile Roads in Washington Township, just south of the Village of Romeo. It is believed that Archibald Powell, shortly before his death in 1836, either sold or donated the property that is now used for the burial ground. (Author's collection.)

The James Thorington family moved to Washington Township around 1819 and lived for about 40 years on a farm on Mound Road in a district known as the Thorington Settlement. Elijah, one of James's sons, was born on January 9, 1809, and passed away on October 5, 1882. Elijah farmed a 240-acre homestead. (Author's collection.)

In 1830, Isaac and Hannah Brabb came to the Territory of Michigan and started a farm across the street from the cemetery. In 1845, James Thorington Jr. provided the land for this burial ground on 31 Mile and Mound Roads. With numerous Brabbs buried here, it eventually was known by the name of the Brabb family. (Author's collection.)

Frederick Snover Crisman owned a 160-acre farm property on the north side of 29 Mile Road. He was the director of the Citizens National Bank of Romeo and held stock in the First National Bank of Romeo. Crissman was an uncompromising abolitionist and a strict advocate of temperance. He died on October 16, 1900, and was buried in Washington Center Cemetery. (Author's collection.)

The Washington Center Cemetery is located on the south side of 29 Mile Road between Campground and Mound Roads. This cemetery is not as large as the other burial grounds in Washington. On June 5, 1848, Henry Moyers sold the half acre to the Township of Washington for use as a burial place. (Author's collection.)

Richard Jersey was born in 1759 in New York. He enlisted to fight in the Revolutionary War and was discharged in 1781. He married Mabel Palmer in 1786, and all six of their children were born in New York. The family came to Michigan in 1824 and homesteaded a parcel of land in Washington until Richard's detain 1831. His grave was marked by the Daughters of the American Revolution in 1941 for recognition for his service. (Author's collection.)

Washington Center is a peaceful burial ground surrounded by trees and iron fencing in the middle of a new residential area. It provides a resting place for many of the early pioneers in this township. Mary Jane Jersey was the first settler to be born in this township, on February 12, 1824; she died on May 22, 1904. (Author's collection.)

Many prominent pioneering families of Washington Township are buried in this cemetery, with the surnames of Jersey, Crissman, Soule, and Stone among them. Otis Lamb and son Edwin are also included. The cemetery has the distinction of having a Revolutionary War soldier buried there, a man named Richard Jersey. (Author's collection.)

Eight

CHANGING TIMES

According to a September 25, 1952, edition of the *Romeo Observer Press*, motorists on Van Dyke Road, upon arriving at the village limits of Washington from the south, were greeted with a roadside sign that read, "Welcome to Washington: A Progressive Community." Just a short distance from this sign was the location of the "92-year-old" Octagon House. It is this contrast, a blend of the historical and modern, that makes Washington one of the most interesting communities in Macomb County. (Courtesy of Melvin E. and Joan D. Bleich Collection, Romeo Community Archives, Romeo District Library.)

Members of the 1945 Washington Card Club are identified, from left to right, as (first row) Lizzy Pierson, Clara Schocke, and Mae Meeker; (second row) Rose Whittemore, Anne Williams, Norma Holstine, Becky Sharp, and Allie Gaskill; (third row) Minnie Vick, Mrs. Kamloske, Mrs. Duncomb, and Hattie Alward. (Courtesy of GWAHS and the John Gaskill Collection.)

The LaChance & Keeler Hardware & Lumber Store on West Road, west of Van Dyke Road, is pictured in the 1930s. A building for unloading lumber supplies for the lumber and hardware company was constructed on the Washington Elevator property where there used to be stock pens on the east side of the railroad tracks. (Courtesy of GWAHS and the Marlene Marsh Collection.)

In 1943, the First Baptist Church of Washington purchased the Weir Block and had it renovated to provide an auditorium on the main floor and living quarters upstairs. In 1956, William Stefanski of Romeo was the owner of the Weir Block; he was also the landlord for the Washington Post Office during the period from 1956 to 1960. The Weir Block continues to be home for many business opportunities to present day. (Both, courtesy of GWATH and the John Gaskill Collection.)

This aerial view shows the area around the elevator in 1950, including the wooden addition that was made in 1947 to the original, long-standing elevator, which sat next to the railway tracks. On the south end of the old feed mill was an irregular-shaped shed. It was probably used as an apple drying room, and it was also known to have been charred on the inside, where it had probably caught fire sometime in the 1920s. The Washington Elevator site and the town of Washington occupied an important place in those days; for many years, income depended on the produce the average farmer sold at what had been termed the Washington Market. (Courtesy of GWAHS and the Dick Bellman Collection.)

In April 1954, many youngsters in the Romeo and Washington areas were given a chance to start their own "Old McDonald's farms," when the Washington Elevator gave away some 2,200 baby chicks to young potential farmers. The baby chick fanciers, from left to right, are James Stark, 12; Dennis Rachow, 5; Judy Rachow, 7; and Johnny Szajna, 6. (Courtesy of Melvin E. and Joan D. Bleich Collection, Romeo Community Archives, Romeo District Library.)

A write-up in the *Romeo Observer Press* of March 12, 1953, states, "The new fire resistant Washington Elevator that had been risen literally from the ashes of the old wooden building that was destroyed in a hundred thousand dollar fire last September, should be complete by the middle of April, and will be one of the most modern elevators in the area." In 2019, the elevator is still a strong part of the community of Washington Township. (Courtesy of Melvin E. and Joan D. Bleich Collection, Romeo Community Archives, Romeo District Library.)

In 1919, Walter Alward Sr. started his business in Washington as a small general store on the east side of Van Dyke Road at West Road. Alward transitioned into the business after having experience as a farmer and an operator of slaughterhouses. Pictured from left to right are unidentified, Lawrence Lambert, Harold Rowley, Walter Alward, and Howard Boldt. (Courtesy of GWAHS and the Fred and Pat Blonde Collection.)

The brick store was rebuilt and expanded four times—three times on the same spot. In 1927, Walter Alward operated a meat market and would move to the west side of Van Dyke, erecting a building with a store on the first floor and living quarters above. Pictured around 1933 are Walter Alward (left) and assistant Arnold Parsons. (Courtesy of GWAHS and the R.J. Brainard Collection.)

This "10 Cents A Loaf!" ad appears in a *Romeo Observer* from 1936. The image was taken at Awards Market in Washington to help promote Wonder Bread. Pictured from left to right are Arnold Parsons, Marguerite Alward, and her little brother Walter. (Courtesy of Melvin E. and Joan D. Bleich Collection, Romeo Community Archives, Romeo District Library.)

10 CENTS A LOAF! This photo was taken in 1936 at Alwards Market in Washington to help promote WONDER BREAD. From left: the late Arnold Parsons, Marguerite Alward and her little brother Walter.

In 1972, Alward's opened a second store on South Main Street in Romeo. In 1986, Alward's moved across Van Dyke Road into a 24,000-square-foot supermarket in Washington; with a 1992 renovation, the size reached 37,000 square feet. Moving the Alward home to a new location on Campground Road made room for more parking. The site is now occupied by the Washington Township Post Office. (Courtesy of Melvin E. and Joan D. Bleich Collection, Romeo Community Archives, Romeo District Library.)

Bellman's Garage was built in 1927 by Irvin Bellman, who operated his garage until his death in 1958. Pictured above are Aldon, Malcomb, and Hilda Bellman. The open bay in the garage was a perfect place for the new volunteer fire department to house its first fire truck. The building still stands today just north of the present-day Weir Block on Van Dyke Road and Wicker Street. (Both, courtesy of GWAHS and the Dick Bellman Collection.)

In this view from the corner of West Road and Van Dyke Road looking north, on the east side, the Weir Block building is home a heating and cooling business, Bellman's is no longer a place to buy gasoline, and Hampton House Furniture is doing business on the west side of Van Dyke. (Courtesy of GWAHS and the Pat Hallman Collection.)

This view looks west from the stoplight at Van Dyke Road onto West Road. On the left, the market has become a restaurant and lounge. The gas station is still where the Cooley house was many years before. (Courtesy of GWAHS and the Pat Hallman Collection.)

The Washington Volunteer Fire Department was established on June 15, 1955. Several disastrous fires that struck the village in the early 1950s prompted several citizens into petitioning the township board for a referendum in the April 1955 election calling for a special assessment district in the south half of the township. The fire department housed in, equipped by, and maintained by Romeo continued to cover the north end of the township, north of 29 Mile Road. During the 1960s, after Romeo decided to cease providing fire service to the northern portions of the township, a vote was held by the township to create a special assessment district that would pay for the costs of providing fire service north of 29 Mile Road. In 1976, the township opened Fire Station No. 2 on 30 Mile Road. (Both, courtesy of Melvin E. and Joan D. Bleich Collection, Romeo Community Archives, Romeo District Library.)

The department's first fire engine was a converted semitruck. Volunteers lengthened the frame of the semi and then purchased and placed a tank on the frame. The volunteers also bought portable pumps and hoses to equip the fire engine. Grade school students raised funds to pay for the siren placed on the vehicle. A women's club purchased the emergency light placed on the top of the engine. 'It was a total community effort," Chief Alward said. In 1974, Gerald Alward was hired as the first full-time chief for the township. The first fire truck was housed in the empty bay at Bellman's garage. (Both, courtesy of Melvin E. and Joan D. Bleich Collection, Romeo Community Archives, Romeo District Library.)

The boulevard that runs horizontally along the bottom portion of this c. 1976 photograph is 26 Mile Road, which is considered the southern border between Washington Township and neighboring Shelby Township. The main road running through Washington was called Main Street, but as time went on, most locals called it "Old Van Dyke Road." Van Dyke Road runs for miles north–south through many communities. (Courtesy of Romeo Community Archives, Romeo District Library.)

Josiah Jewell from Genesee County, New York, purchased 160 acres of government land on June 8, 1825. The 160 acres spanned the entire front portion of land running from 28 Mile to 29 Mile on Mound Road. By 1859, Jackson Crissman owned those 160 acres, configured differently, and then added 75 additional acres for a total of 235. The property stayed with the Crissman family until Jackson's death in 1881 and his wife, Mary, in 1902. By 1916, the property had a new owner in William Hart, who picked up an additional five acres; he remained the owner into the 1930s. By 1982, Stanley Ross had owned the land for some years, and it was worked as the Maxwell Dairy Farm. By 2001, the land again moved into private hands. The property now is home to the Stonycreek Veterinary Hospital. (Both, courtesy of GWAHS and the Pat Hallman Collection.)

Washington Township was on the Grand Trunk Western Railroad, later called the Romeo Subdivision, which was six miles southwest of Romeo. The rail system was for many years very important to the Washington Elevator's business. By 1966, long after the trains discontinued the Washington run, Bob Owens purchased the unused rail station and, with extensive remodeling, brought the structure back to life as a museum. (Both, courtesy of GWAHS.)

In 1999, the Grand Trunk Railway had workmen digging up rails adjacent to the Washington Elevator on West Road as crews continued to pull up the abandoned tracks from Washington through to Romeo. Service had stopped on the 120-year-old rail line many years before Macomb County Parks and Recreation had plans for the historic line to be turned into a hiking trail. (Courtesy of Melvin E. and Joan D. Bleich Collection, Romeo Community Archives, Romeo District Library.)

In 1966, Bob Owen, with a lifelong love of trains, purchased the Washington Grand Truck Railway depot building for $200. It was moved three miles from its location on West Street, near the elevator, to 29 Mile and Van Dyke Roads and became the Whistle Stop Museum. Travelers could not help but stare when passing the shop, a restored converted railroad depot with its outside collection of antique railcars. (Courtesy of Melvin E. and Joan D. Bleich Collection, Romeo Community Archives, Romeo District Library.)

Beginning in the 1950s, much of the farmland was sold off and converted to subdivisions of new homes, as seen in this c. 1952 image of one of the rapidly growing areas in Washington, with new homes already completed—and more on the drawing boards. There were also many new roads connecting these subdivisions north and south of 26 Mile Road. (Courtesy of Melvin E. and Joan D. Bleich Collection, Romeo Community Archives, Romeo District Library.)

Located on the north side of 26 Mile Road, just east of Mound Road, the Johnny Appleseed Cider Mill, which opened around 1984, was a family-owned business. In the fall season, the mill offered a rustic setting where customers could at times watch the cider-making process. Pictured here from left to right are co-owner Kathy Berg with Mildred Holtkamp and Laura Venable, workers at the mill. (Courtesy of Melvin E. and Joan D. Bleich Collection, Romeo Community Archives, Romeo District Library.)

On October 3, 1825, Henry Moyers (Moires) purchased 80 acres that this home would eventually be built on, and a half-acre of that land Henry was sold to the Township of Washington for use as a burial place, Washington Center Cemetery. Gilbert Moyers, Henry's son, became the next owner of the land, and in 1863 the farm and house were deeded to his brother Joseph for a dollar. The home ultimately sat on 120 acres. After many years and various owners, the house was moved (to avoid demolition) in 2003 to make way for a golf course and condominiums. The home was moved from 29 Mile Road and placed on property on Campground Road, right around the corner from its previous site. (Both, courtesy of Melvin E. and Joan D. Bleich Collection, Romeo Community Archives, Romeo District Library.)

As stated in the May 25, 1950, *Romeo Observer*, "Washington Township's new office building and township hall sits on Rawles Street, between Lafayette and Washington Streets. The 25-by-50-foot building is a gem of early American architecture, in keeping with the original flavor of the Romeo area. It houses all affairs of the Romeo area of Washington Township, including all elections. Later in 1950, the board asked for bids for a second building in the village of Washington to hold offices and services for the Washington area." (Courtesy of Melvin E. and Joan D. Bleich Collection, Romeo Community Archives, Romeo District Library.)

April 1991 saw the Washington Township open its new municipal building for business interests in the community. Plans for the hall, located on Van Dyke Road between West Road and 26 Mile Road, date back to the mid-1980s when a committee was formed to investigate possible sites for a new township hall. Along with township offices, there is an Older Adult Center, and the library was housed there until the Graubner Library opened in 2001. (Courtesy of GWAHS and the R.J Brainard Collection.)

The Washington Historical Museum is in the old Washington High School. The school was built in 1916, and classes were held in this building until 1972. The museum was first established in 1975. Through the years, many hardworking and very dedicated people worked to preserve the many historical items left in the care of the museum for Washington Township. (Courtesy of GWAHS.)

Similar to the Romeo Township Hall built shortly before, this Township Hall was built to handle the business concerns of the Washington Township area. The structure located off Van Dyke Road and Pilgrim Street also housed the 600-square-foot Washington Branch of the Romeo District Library. A new, 2,600-square-foot library, featuring the latest technology, broke ground in 2000 on land donated by the Graubner family. (Courtesy of Melvin E. and Joan D. Bleich Collection, Romeo Community Archives, Romeo District Library.)

Built on an old gravel quarry, the Greystone Golf Club was founded in 1992. The area boasts spectacular views and rolling hills. When the lands grants were first up for sale, Michael Hopkins, from New York, purchased 80 acres on May 27, 1825, and with Hannah Brabb, from Macomb County, purchased the adjoining property on January 21, 1836. Most of this property would stay in the Brabb family for the next 100 years. (Courtesy of GWAHS and R.J. Brainard Collection.)

The Orchards Golf Club and the residential golf community that surrounds it run along Campground Road. Marquis Nye would purchase the south 80 acres on June 1822, and Aaron Stone would purchase the north 80 acres of government land on October 22, 1822. All the property between 28 and 29 on Campground Road would be in the Stone family soon and then pass into the Couch family. (Courtesy of GWAHS and the R.J. Brainard Collection.)

The Glacier Club opened in 1993 and was originally designed by Bill Newcomb. The grounds were renovated by a renowned golf course architect named Arthur Hills in 2008. Edwin Lamb, an early settler to the Washington area, built the house in 1860 that the Glacier Club later used as a clubhouse. A golfing community of homes was added as part of the Glacier Club, located on Glacier Club Drive, off of Campground Road, at the fork near Van Dyke Road. (Both, courtesy of GWAHS and the R.J. Brainard Collection.)

A casual traveler, noting the glistening new elementary school and the modern dwellings dotting the village, would never guess the humble beginnings of this pioneering community. An article in the September 25, 1952, *Romeo Observer Press* cites a historian writing as far back as 1882: "Large well-cultivated fields, nice residences and splendid roads are now to be seen on every hand, instead of Indian encampments, trails and dense forests. And the trials and privations endured by those early, hardy settlers are, by the present generation in their abundance, scarcely remembered." (Courtesy of Melvin E. and Joan D. Bleich Collection, Romeo Community Archives, Romeo District Library.)

BIBLIOGRAPHY

Allen, Robert D. and Cheryl J. *The Andrus Family: A Pioneer Family of Washington Township, Michigan*. A Bit of Washington History. Self-published, Romeo Printing, 2006.

———. *The Cemeteries of Washington Township*. A Bit of Washington History. Self-published, Romeo Printing, 2016.

———. *The Cannon Family & "Gods Acre": The History of a Michigan Pioneer Family*. Self-published, 2013.

———. *Dr. Albert Yates, The County Doctor*. A Bit of Washington History. Self-published, Romeo Printing, 2015.

———. *The Octagon Houses*. A Bit of Washington History. Self-published, Romeo Printing, 2015.

———. *Washington Cemetery: History Rests Here*. Self-published, 2009.

Anders, Judith A. *The Loren Andrus Octagon House 1860 Washington, Michigan: Myths, Facts, and Legends*. Grand Rapids, MI: Color House Graphics 2003.

Burt, John S. *They Left Their Mark: William Austin Burt and His Sons Surveyors of the Public Domain*. Rancho Cordova, CA: Landmark Enterprises, 1985.

Buzzelli, Elizabeth Kane. *A History of Romeo Community School District, 1824–1976*. Ann Arbor, MI: Edwards Brothers, 1976.

Eldredge, Robert F. *Past and Present of Macomb County, Michigan*. Chicago: S.J. Clarke, 1905.

Greater Washington Township Historical Society. *Through These Doors*. Washington, MI: Greater Washington Historical Society. 1972.

Leeson, Michael A. *History of Macomb County*. Chicago: M.A. Leeson, 1882.

McLaughlin, David. *Romeo*. Images of America. Charleston, SC: Arcadia Publishing, 2004.

DISCOVER THOUSANDS OF LOCAL HISTORY BOOKS FEATURING MILLIONS OF VINTAGE IMAGES

Arcadia Publishing, the leading local history publisher in the United States, is committed to making history accessible and meaningful through publishing books that celebrate and preserve the heritage of America's people and places.

Find more books like this at
www.arcadiapublishing.com

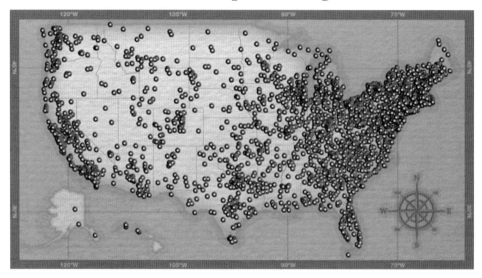

Search for your hometown history, your old stomping grounds, and even your favorite sports team.

Consistent with our mission to preserve history on a local level, this book was printed in South Carolina on American-made paper and manufactured entirely in the United States. Products carrying the accredited Forest Stewardship Council (FSC) label are printed on 100 percent FSC-certified paper.